City of Derry

An Illustrated
History and Companion for Londonderry

Paintings by
Pat Cowley

Text by
Brian Lacey B.A. Hons.

Cottage

Publications

First published by Cottage Publications,
Donaghadee N. Ireland 1995.
Copyrights Reserved
© Illustrations by Pat Cowley 1995
© Text by Brian Lacey 1995
All rights reserved.
Printed in Singapore

ISBN 0 9516402 7 5

List of Contents

The Artist

A Derry man born and bred, Pat Cowley still lives and works in the city with his wife and young family. Continuing a lifelong interest in painting he trained in art at Belfast College of Art, before graduating from the University of Ulster at Coleraine to return to Derry where he is now Head of the Art Department at St. Peter's High School.

Whether in oil or watercolour Pat's paintings of Derry and Donegal are highly regarded not only locally but also internationally and he has exhibited widely, both in solo and group exhibitions in places as far apart as New York, Toronto and London.

The Author

Although born in Dublin, Brian Lacey has spent most of his working life exploring and documenting the history of the northwest corner of Ireland. After studying Celtic Archaeology and early Irish History at University College Dublin, he directed a series of excavations at sites in the centre of Derry in the 1970's and oversaw the Donegal Archaeological Survey in 1980-81. A regular contributer to historical publications, he edited the Archaeological Survey of County Donegal published in 1983. More recent books include Historic Derry (1988), The Seige of Derry (1989) and Seige City - The Story of Derry and Londonderry (1990). As head of Derry City Council's Museum Service he had primary responsibility for developing and setting up the City's award winning Tower Museum.

"If Stones Could Speak"

In the foyer of St. Columb's Cathedral, on the highest point of the hill on which the old city of Derry is built, there is a small foundation stone inscribed with a famous verse:–

> "If stones could speake
> Then London's prayse
> Should sounde who
> Built this church and
> Cittie from the ground"

The verse commemorates the part played by various institutions of the City of London in the construction of the cathedral and the foundation of the walled City of Londonderry in the early seventeenth century. However, by that stage Derry was already a very ancient place, with a recorded history going back a thousand years, and a series of legends which pushed its story back even further.

The fact that in modern times the city is known by two names reflects this dual origin. Throughout its long history it has been known by many names, not only by two as is commonly assumed. Daire Calgach; Roboretum Calgachi; Doire Cholmcille; Derry and Londonderry, and as many as over fifty variations and versions of all of these have been in use at different times. One thing all these names have in common, however, whether in the original Irish variations or in their anglicised or Latin versions, is the place name element 'Derry' (in the Irish language – Daire or Doire). Derry means an oak grove, or, perhaps more correctly in this instance, an oak-tree covered hillside.

Oak trees and oak groves had a special significance in the religious and ritual lives of the Celtic people of ancient times. This was by no means confined to Ireland and oak tree place names similar to 'derry' are found widespread in western Europe, wherever the Celts settled or travelled. For example, the first part of the name of the Adriatic city of Dubrovnik seems to come from the same ancient root word, as probably also does the word Druid and draoichta, the word in Irish for magic.

Archaeological objects and sites dating back to the Stone Age (7500–2000 B.C.) and the succeeding Bronze Age have been found on many occasions within the confines of the modern city limits. New material dating from these periods is constantly coming to light, especially along the banks of the River Foyle, showing us that the area was fairly well populated even in remote, prehistoric times.

Perhaps the best known legend about the foundation of Derry tells us how a monastery came to be established there about the middle or second half of the 6th century. The year traditionally assigned for this event is A.D. 546, although historians now think that it unlikely that this is the correct date it is probably not too wide of the mark.

The stories tell us that Colm Cille, who was born at Gartan in modern Donegal in 521 into a local ruling family, had gone from his birthplace to study at the monastery of Glasnevin, now on the outskirts of Dublin. When a major plague broke out the monks were sent back to their homelands for their protection. Colm Cille arrived in Derry on the borders of his peoples' territories where his cousin, the local king Aed mac Ainmire, had a fortress. The king gave this fortress and the surrounding land to Colm Cille, so that a Christian monastery might be built there. Everyone was astonished when the first thing that the holy man did was to set fire to the place in order, as he claimed, to erase "the works of worldly men that he might consecrate it to God and to himself".

According to legend the fire grew so fierce that it threatened to burn down the surrounding oak grove from which the place was named. However, Colm Cille pronounced a prayer in Latin, Noli Pater Indulgere, and immediately the fire subsided and the trees were saved. It is said that this prayer can still protect people from fire and lightning. While it is clear that these legendary stories are not historical they nevertheless suggest that some kind of rite of exorcism may have been necessary before this pagan ritual place would be suitable for the building of a Christian community.

Many of the legends about the foundation of the monastery of Derry stress how much Colm Cille loved its trees. One little poem, the original of which is in Irish and which a much later writer puts into the mouth of the saint, tells of the degree of that love.

> "Though truly I'm afraid
> Of death itself and Hell
> I'm frankly more afraid
> Of an axe-sound, west in Derry".

These stories are given a Christian veneer but it is clear that their true significance lies in the ritual importance of those trees in pagan times. The repeated writing down of these legends shows us that this sense of taboo about interfering with the trees of Derry continued right down through history, until at least the 16th century.

However despite the weight of legend, more reliable historical evidence about the beginnings of the monastery, although itself somewhat confused, suggests that another man, Fiachrach mac Ciarain (who died in 620) might have had a greater, if not sole involvement in the foundation of the monastery of Derry. As one wry modern commentator has remarked about Colm Cille's reputation in this regard, "this wouldn't be the only instance in the history of the city when someone got the credit for a job they didn't do!" However in spite of the claims of Fiachrach, it is the feast day (the anniversary of his death) of Colm Cille on 9th June, which is still popularly commemorated in Derry and in popular lore it is always Colm Cille who is credited with the foundation of the city.

There is also some dispute about the location of the original monastic buildings. Tradition tends to favour the area around the Long Tower church (named from the round tower built there in medieval times), while modern research would tend to favour the area around St. Augustine's Church of Ireland chapel-of-ease.

At its foundation the monastery of Derry would have been a fairly small settlement. We have no direct evidence as to what it looked like but originally it probably consisted of a collection of circular dwelling huts and workshops, along with a rectangular wooden church inside a protective, circular enclosing wall or fence.

One of the stories in the legends tells us about the monks of Derry being sent by Colm Cille into the nearby woods to cut young stakes or wattles for the buildings. The wattles were on the land of a young man who lived beside the monastery. He was annoyed that the wood was cut without his permission. When Colm Cille heard of his anger he told his monks to bring the man the value of his wood in barley grain and tell him to sew it in the ground. Although it was already the middle of summer the man planted it and, miraculously, the grain grew. It was ripe by the beginning of August.

Gradually the monastery of Derry would have grown larger, with a few hundred monks and probably a number of lay people living around its edge. It 'belonged' to the people known as the Cenel Conaill, the family of which both Colm Cille and Fiachrach mac Ciarain were members. The name of these people survives to the present in the form Tyrconnel.

No ancient manuscripts survive from Derry. However, there are frequent references to the former existence of such documents in early historical records: the Book of Derry contained genealogical information, and the Gospel Book of Saint Martin was one of the great treasures of the monastery of Derry. The latter was probably a beautifully illuminated manuscript similar to the other well-known gospel books associated with Colm Cille, the Book of Durrow and the Book of Kells.

Throughout the first few centuries of its existence the monastery of Derry seems to have been a small, quiet institution. A party of vikings were defeated in a battle there in 833 by the important local king Nial Caille. Another group of vikings plundered the monastery in 990 and again, perhaps, in 997.

Derry was to get an enormous boost when the powerful provincial king, Domnall Mac Lochlainn, succeeded in 1083. Domnall made Derry the seat or capital of his dynasty, and began developing the secular township which was already growing around the monastery. When he died in Derry on 9th February 1121, his obituarist claimed that he was high-king of Ireland, and boasted that he "was the most distinguished of the Gael for form and birth, for good sense and prowess, for happiness and prosperity, for giving away treasure and food".

The settlement, which by this stage must have been as near to being a town as anything was in Gaelic Ireland, thrived. Throughout the 12th century the contemporary documents give us a glimpse of the tempestuous secular and ecclesiastical life of Derry.

One of the greatest figures to dominate the life of Derry in the 12th century was the abbot Flaithbertach O'Brolchain who died in 1175. Flaithbertach made Derry the headquarters of all the churches in Ireland which claimed to have been founded by St. Colm Cille.

He also built, in 1164, the Tempull Mor (literally – the great church) which in the following century was to become a cathedral when Derry was named as the centre of a diocese. The Tempull Mor, which was located near the site of the Long Tower church, was to give its name (in the anglicised form Templemore) to many of the city's modern institutions.

The 12th and 13th centuries were the great days of medieval Derry. The Augustinian rule was introduced for the existing monks and a separate Dominican Priory was established. The lay community prospered and we read of pilgrimages and visits to the settlement by kings and chieftains from other parts of Ireland. In 1197 the Normans made several expeditions to Derry, led on at least two occasions by their great lord, John de Courcy. Other Norman and Normanised families, such as the Mac Uchtreds and the de Burgos, were later granted land in Derry by the King of England.

It is a member of the de Burgo family, Walter, who is said to be represented by the skeleton or figure of death on the city's coat-of-arms. Walter is said to have been immured (literally blocked up in a recess in a wall) by his brother, in the course of a family dispute at Greencastle in County Donegal, and to have died by starvation in the year 1332. There are many other local, popular explanations for the heraldic skeleton. Most of these centre on the claim that he represents a citizen kept waiting by bureaucracy.

The first recorded visit of an Englishman to Derry occurred in 1397 with the arrival of John Colton, the Archbishop of Armagh. Colton is the only person in Irish history to have held the two senior ecclesiastical and lay posts in the country. For a short period in 1382 before becoming head of the church, he had been appointed justiciar or head of the King's government in Ireland. Colton's colourful caravan, which included fifteen other important Gaelic and Anglo-Norman ecclesiastics and their attendants, set out from Armagh on a cool autumn morning. They took two days to travel over the Sperrin mountains and on to Derry by horseback and ferryboat. We can gain an interesting feel of the time because the party also included a secretary who kept a careful record of the journey.

When they got to Derry on 10th October all the monks, clergy and laymen came out to greet these important visitors. However, it quickly became apparent that moral discipline, especially among the monks, was not as tight as it might be. As well as conducting a series of religious services and ceremonies, including a hugely-attended open air eucharist in what is now the grounds of St. Colm's park in the Waterside area of the city, the archbishop had to preside at a number of ecclesiastical courts and lay down a set of rules for the better conduct of the monastery. He ordered the abbot, Brother Hugh Mac Gillibride O'Doherty "within the space of three days, to dismiss and send away from your presence, cohabitation and care, never to take her back, that Catherine O'Doherty, whom you have lately taken as a concubine". Never again was Brother Hugh to give goods to, or promise to look after, a concubine and he was also to restore to the monastery any of its property which he had previously given to Catherine as presents!

Sometime around 1500 the O'Doherty chieftains bought a piece of land in Derry from the Mac Lochlainn family, for which they paid the sum of twenty cows. In lieu of certain taxes, the O'Doherty's built a small castle there for their overlords the O'Donnells, who by now ruled the area. That castle survived well into the 17th century and was used as the ammunition and gunpowder magazine for the plantation city. Today, the former existence of this castle is recalled by the O'Doherty tower, built in 1986, which forms part of the award-winning Tower Museum.

In the autumn of 1566, an English force of about one thousand men sailed from Bristol and landed in Derry. They were part of a great military pincer movement designed to overthrow the Ulster chieftain Shane O'Neill. The other half of the force marched northwards overland from Dublin. Derry was chosen as the location for a garrison as it lay on the border of O'Neill's territory and on the River Foyle, which effectively acted as a water highway into the heart of Gaelic Ulster. However, the English troops quickly fell victim to the damp climate of north-western Ireland and an explosion in their gun-powder store brought about an end to this first attempt by the English to capture Derry. It was not until 1600 that another attempt was made.

In May of that year, during the Nine Years War against the leaders of Gaelic Ulster, a force led by Henry Docwra landed at Derry and succeeded in establishing and maintaining a garrison there until the end of hostilities in 1603. With the war over, in 1604 King James I, finding that "The town or borough of Derrie is, by reason of the natural seat and situation thereof, a place very convenient and fit to be made both a town of war and a town of merchandise ...." granted it a charter with city status.

The small settlement began to grow again and the first Protestant bishop, George Montgomery, was appointed. His wife, writing to her sister, prayed that the pleasant-sounding Derry would "make us all merry". However, in 1608 the local chieftain Sir Cahir O'Doherty, who previously had supported the English and been a burgess (councillor) of the infant city, rebelled and burnt the small settlement. A contemporary lamented that "it was the fairest begun city that ever was made in so short a time, and so well seated upon a goodly river".

But its destruction laid the foundation for a new chapter in its history. In 1609 'four wise, grave and discreet' citizens of London came over to inspect the territories which the 'City' was granted as part of the plantations in Ulster. The special body set up in London to oversee this development, The Honourable The Irish Society, still survives and is involved in the life of Derry to this day. A walled city was planned as the jewel in the crown of the new colony. Work began, and in 1613 it was renamed Londonderry. By 1618 the famous walls were built and slowly the population rose with new settlers coming from England and, especially, from Scotland.

During the turbulent years of the 1640's when war and civil war convulsed both Britain and Ireland, Londonderry became a refuge for many of the settlers in Ulster. However, contrary to much opinion, it was not attacked by the native Irish. In fact the first siege of Derry in 1649 occurred when Presbyterian forces loyal to the crown rose up against and besieged their fellow Protestants inside the city who supported the parliamentary side in the English Civil War. The ultimate irony was that on this occasion the city was relieved by the Catholic and native Irish force led by Owen Roe O'Neill.

In the quieter years following the 'Restoration' of King Charles II, a boy was born in the city who was to achieve great fame. That boy, who was later to become known as the dramatist George Farquhar (1677-1707), also attended the local Free School, the ancestor of today's Foyle and Londonderry College.

By 1688 about 2000 people were living in the city, almost all of them inside its walls and almost all of them Protestant. These people were prey to various rumours of impending disaster which were sweeping the land as a result of the changes being introduced by the Roman Catholic King, James II, who had succeeded in 1685.

On December 7th (18th by our reckoning, as the calendar has since been adjusted by 11 days) 1688, a contingent of the Earl of Antrim's soldiers, known as the Redshank's, arrived in Derry to take over as garrison. The troops were Catholic and the townspeople feared that the soldiers had come to massacre them. A group of the younger and more radical people, 'the apprentice boys', closed the city gates and prevented the entry of these troops. In the months which followed the citizens hardened their position and switched their support to the new Protestant king, William III, who had taken over the throne from James.

James came to Ireland to use it as a base to recapture his throne and all Catholic Ireland rallied to his cause. Only Londonderry, and a few other places in Ulster, held out against him. James came to Londonderry on April 18th 1689 to find a citizens' army which refused him entry. Some of the garrison even fired at the king. While James himself despondently left the area, his troops, including British, Irish and French contingents, blockaded the city and began to attack it. The Siege of Derry was to last for 105 days and, before it was over, was to include appalling episodes of violence and heroism, of suffering and humanitarian concern.

On August 1st (or 12th) 1689, Williamite relief ships broke through a barrier or boom which had been stretched across the river downstream (just beyond the location of the present Foyle Bridge), precisely to prevent such ships and their supplies reaching the beleaguered city. The 'breaking of the boom' brought the siege to an end but the war between the two kings was continued elsewhere in Ireland, most notably two years later at the Battle of the Boyne. The siege left an enormous impression on the Protestant citizens of the city, both in the short and long terms. Echoes of those times can still be found in the buildings, the institutions, the commemorations, and even the politics of the city.

In the aftermath of the siege the city had to be rebuilt. Some of the elegant Georgian architecture of those days still graces the city's streets. The traveller Arthur Young who came in the 1770's described the city at that time as "the most picturesque of any place I have seen". The great 18th century ecclesiastic and philosopher

George Berkeley was Dean of Derry from 1724 to 1733. However, it was another cleric, Frederick Augustus Hervey, Earl of Bristol and Church of Ireland Bishop of Derry (1768-1803), who made an even greater impression.

Hervey was an eccentric but also a very practical man. He was a great builder, a collector of antiquities and works of art, a well-known traveller and an ecumenist. He cared for the material as well as the spiritual needs of all the people of his diocese both Catholic and Protestant. His campaign to see a bridge built across the Foyle at Derry ranks as one of his most noteworthy contributions to the city. The bridge, the city's first, was opened in 1791.

In the 18th century the population of the city grew by a factor of almost four to 11 000. By the end of the 19th century it had grown four times again, and by the outbreak of the First World War it had reached about 45 000. This had happened for a number of reasons but a lot of the additional people had come into the city from its rural hinterland, especially Donegal, in pursuit of the jobs provided by the industrialisation and expansion of the city. The city was now developing well outside its 17th century walls and along both sides of the river.

Grand public buildings were erected. Impressive factories dotted the city (many of which still survive) and large warehouses stretched along the riverside and quays. New working class and middle class suburbs were built. Shirt manufacturing became the dominant industry following the invention of the portable sewing machine in America in the 1840s. By the time the industry reached its peak in the 1920s, it employed 18 000 people, most of them women.

The city's quays had been busy since the 17th century but in the 18th century they acquired an additional export item – people. Emigration, especially of Presbyterians (the Ulster-Scots) to North

America, began in the early 18th century. In the 19th century, emigration was largely from the Catholic community, particularly in the aftermath of the Great Famine of the 1840s. As one of the most westerly ports in Europe, Derry 'Kay' (quay) played an especially important role in the emigration 'trade'. Many of the great sailing ships, like the well-loved Minnehaha, were owned by local businessmen and the servicing and provisioning of these ships and their passengers was an important aspect of the local economy.

The coming of the railway in 1847 had a significant impact on the life of the city and its communications with other centres. Eventually Derry was to have four railway networks emanating from the city, each with its own terminal. The lines were joined by the lower, 'railway' deck of the unusual two-tier Carlisle Bridge (built in 1863) and its successor, the Craigavon Bridge, built in 1933. In 1984 the city acquired a second river crossing, the elegant Foyle Bridge which, at the time of its construction, was the longest bridge in Ireland.

For the most part, it would probably have to be admitted that the 20th century has not been the kindest period of the city's history. The impact of partition, economic decline and stagnation, unemployment, emigration, political difficulties and, not least, 'the troubles' have all taken their toll. Yet despite all this the population has doubled since 1900.

Paradoxically, one of the high points of the century for the city was during the Second World War. There was plenty of employment, a bustling cosmopolitan atmosphere and a touch of glamour generated by the foreign servicemen based in the city. There were casualties on only one occasion when fifteen people were killed by bombs dropped in April 1941. The city played an important part in the allied war effort. According to one historian it held 'the key to victory in the Atlantic'. In a gesture to honour this, the port of

Lisahally, just outside the city, was nominated for the surrender of part of the German U-boat fleet at the end of the war.

'The troubles' proved devastating. At one point it was said that as much as one third of the 'downtown' area of the city had been destroyed. But the city survived and, from the beginning of the 1980's especially, a vibrant programme of physical and social reconstruction could be discerned. In 1988 an independent survey conducted for the BBC judged that Derry was "one of the ten best places to live in, in the United Kingdom". The criteria were based on an assessment of the quality of life and on the quality of the local environment.

Nobody would say that the city is without problems, but it is also a place of great optimism, energy and imaginative independence. There can be little doubt, in the words of one of the best-known songs about the city, that there "is a bright brand-new day" in store for this ancient and fascinating place.

Important Events in the History of the City

546	Traditional date of foundation of monastery by St. Colm Cille / Columba.
620	Death of Fiachrach, the 'other founder' of Derry.
724	Death of Caech Scuili, the scribe of Derry.
833	Irish victory over the Vikings at Derry.
990	Derry plundered by Vikings.
c.1100	Derry becomes 'capital' of MacLochlainn dynasty.
1164	The Tempul Mor (great church) built in Derry.
1197	The Normans visit Derry for the first time.
1247	Derry recognised as the seat of a diocese.
1311	Derry granted to the Norman de Burgos by Edward II.
1469	Papal Indulgence granted to all who assist in restoration of the Tempul Mor – 'the cathedral church of Derry'.
1566	First English occupation of Derry. Lasts six months.
1600	English capture Derry for the second time.
1604	Grant of charter to city of 'Derrie'.
1608	Derry burned by Sir Cahir O'Doherty.
1613	Charter of Londonderry granted by James I.
1633	St. Columb's Cathedral built.
1649	First Siege.
1688	'Shutting of the Gates'.
1689	Siege of Derry.
1718	Beginnings of emigration to America.
1768	Frederick Augustus Hervey, 'the Earl Bishop' appointed.

1772	Londonderry Journal established.
1784	Long Tower Church begun.
1791	First bridge across the Foyle opened.
1829	Londonderry Sentinel begins publishing.
1830	Shirt industry established around this time.
1847	Railways begin operating from the city.
1857	Tillie and Henderson's shirt factory opened.
1863	Double-deck Carlisle Bridge built.
1865	Magee College founded.
1896	McCorkell shipping business closes signalling the end of Derry sailing ships.
1912	Present Guildhall rebuilt after fire of 1908.
1920	First Nationalist mayor elected.
1932	Amelia Earhart, first women, solo trans-Atlantic pilot lands near Derry.
1941	'US Naval Operating base, Londonderry' built.
1945	Surrender of German U-Boats at Lisahally.
1969	Start of the 'troubles'.
1973	Londonderry District Council set up.
1978	Inner City Trust begins regeneration work.
1992	Port of Londonderry moves to Lisahally.
1994/5	Major re-development of Foyleside.

PAT COWLEY

Name and Address

Telephone

THE FERRYQUAY GATE

Originally the walled city had only four gates. The principal one opened out onto the river at the 'ship quay' where large boats tied up. A separate gate on the eastern side of the city led to the 'ferry quay'. The ferry was the only means of crossing the river until 1790 when the first bridge was built. It was the Ferryquay Gate which was slammed shut in December 1688 by the apprentice boys against a detachment of the Earl of Antrim's troops, known as the Redshanks, thus beginning the Siege. The original wooden gate was replaced in 1865 by the present stone archway which is decorated with stone heads of the Revs. George Walker and James Gordon, two heroes of the Siege.

With thanks to The Honourable The Irish Society

B

Name and Address	Telephone

THE APPRENTICE BOYS HALL

The Memorial Hall, as it is often called, is the headquarters of the Apprentice Boys of Derry. The precursor of this body was set up in 1814 to commemorate the events of the Siege of 1689 and in particular the actions of thirteen 'resolute apprentice boys'. On 7th December 1688 these young men shut the gates of the city against the advance of a detachment of the Earl of Antrim's troops who were loyal to King James II. The hall was built in 1873 to a design by John Guy Ferguson, one of the best known architects and public figures of his day in the city. Extended in 1937, the Memorial Hall contains rooms for private meetings, some social facilities and a small museum.

With thanks to W.J. Sproule

PAT COWLEY

Name and Address	Telephone

THE CITY FROM THE LETTERKENNY ROAD

One of the simplest aspects of the city's past is its geology. The underlying rock skeleton of the land is made up of just one type of stone; the local variety of schist. Formed as horizontal layers five hundred million years ago, it was later folded into a series of hills and valleys which, although modified greatly during the Ice Ages, have survived to the present. The River Foyle flows in one of these valleys around three sides of the hill of Derry. Originally it also ran along the valley forming the fourth (western) side but about 3000 B.C. the water level fell and the valley left what is known today as 'The Bogside' as a marshy boggy area. As late as the 17th century Derry was still called 'the island'.

With thanks to L.P.C. Stationery

PAT COWLEY

Name and Address	*Telephone*

THE LONG TOWER CHURCH

The Long Tower Church was originally built in a much simplified manner in 1784, the first Roman Catholic church in the city following the Reformation and the Plantations. Auspiciously the city's Protestants, including the Bishop, made a contribution to its construction. It takes its name from the ancient monastic round (or 'long') tower which stood nearby until well into the 17th century. The great 12th century church, the Tempull Mor, also stood near here. The Long Tower Church was effectively rebuilt in 1909, and decorated in a rich neo-renaissance style. The building in the foreground once housed Hasson's old forge, for many years a well known city landmark.

PAT COWLEY

Name and Address	Telephone

SPENCER ROAD

Spencer Road, with its pleasant mix of shops and small businesses, is the main shopping street in the Waterside area of the city. Running parallel to the river for most of its length, the southern end of Spencer Road turns abruptly towards the Craigavon Bridge while to the east the land rises steeply towards the Top of the Hill and Gobnascale areas with their magnificent views over the City. Before the 19th century the Waterside area was little more than a cluster of houses but the building of the new Ebrington Barracks in 1839 and the coming of the railway to Coleraine in 1853, paved the way for the extensive development of this suburb of the city.

With thanks to Hills (Derry) Ltd.

Name and Address	*Telephone*

No. 6 and 8 Shipquay Street

The Siege of 1689 resulted in the destruction of many of the buildings inside the walled city. Rebuilding commenced almost immediately and throughout the 18th century the streets were adorned with fine Georgian houses which functioned both as dwellings and places of business. A number of these elegant structures still survive, such as this adjoining pair near the top of Shipquay Street. No. 6 with its beautiful doorway probably dates to the middle of the 18th century while No. 8 may have been built a short time later. For a while in the 19th century Colonel Thomas Colby, Director of the first Ordnance Survey of Ireland, lived in this house.

With thanks to The McGilloway Gallery

PAT COWLEY

Name and Address	Telephone

THE GRIANAN OF AILEACH

The Grianan of Aileach is a hilltop complex of ancient monuments which spans the period from probably the late Stone Age (around 4000 BC) down to our own times. The oldest structure, unfortunately now gone, was probably a tomb dating to the Neolithic or early Bronze Age period. The whole site is enclosed by a set of earthen banks forming a hillfort of the late Bronze Age (perhaps 1000 B.C.). However, the most impressive structure is the circular fortification or 'cashel' which lies at the centre of the complex. This was one of the chief dwelling places of the northern Ui Neill dynasty which gave kings and leaders to Gaelic Ulster from the 6th to the 12th century and beyond.

With thanks to Bookworm Community Bookshop

PAT COWLEY

Name and Address	*Telephone*

TILLIE AND HENDERSON'S FACTORY AND 'HANDS ACROSS THE DIVIDE'

In 1992 a new sculpture was erected at the western end of Craigavon Bridge. The bronze statues and small garden called 'Hands Across the Divide' is by a local sculptor, Maurice Harron. Behind the sculpture can be seen Tillie and Henderson's former shirt factory building. About 1830 William Scott, a local businessman, began making shirts in Derry. However it was not until the invention of the portable sewing machine around 1845, and its introduction to the city in the 1850s by William Tillie and John Henderson, that the industry began its major expansion. This building has the distinction of being mentioned by Karl Marx in Das Kapital.

With thanks to Derry Boston Ventures Ltd.

I

Name and Address   Telephone

CARLISLE ROAD

Carlisle Road is a lively city street with lots of small businesses, which descends gently from the Ferryquay Gate on the eastern section of the city walls down towards the Craigavon Bridge. The street was not laid out until the 1860s when it became necessary as a result of the construction of the Carlisle Bridge, opened in 1863. The street still retains much of its 19th century character. The only break in the continuous line of buildings on the left-hand side is the site of the former Opera House. Carlisle Road used to be a favourite promenade for young people interested in 'eyeing-up' the opposite gender.

With thanks to Moore's of Derry

PAT COWLEY

Name and Address	Telephone

The River Foyle from Prehen Boathouse

The Foyle is formed some fifteen miles above the city by the Mourne and Finn Rivers when they come together between the towns of Lifford and Strabane. Flowing past the city in a graceful curve, it continues for another five miles before passing Culmore Point, out into the oval-shaped Lough Foyle and on into the Atlantic Ocean. Only 1000 feet wide at Craigavon Bridge, at Rosses Bay, inside the city limits, it is as much as 1 1/4 miles across. The river and lough take their name from the mythical character Feabhal mac Lodan. According to legend, when the lough was forming it drowned Feabhal and cast his body on the shore, along with a stone to act as his burial monument.

With thanks to The Richmond Centre

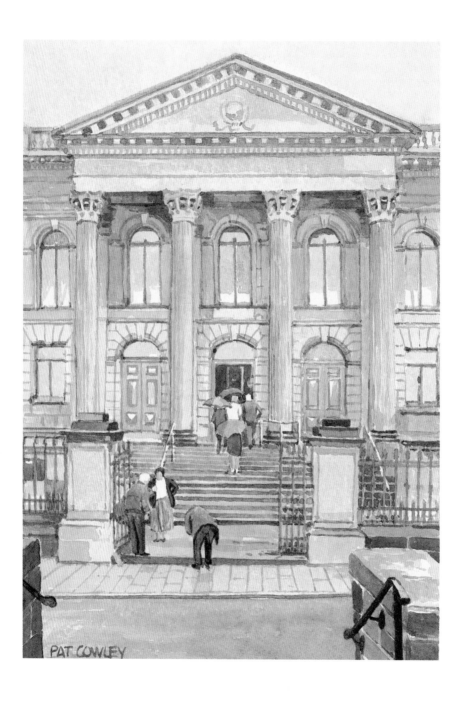

PAT COWLEY

Name and Address

Telephone

FIRST DERRY PRESBYTERIAN CHURCH

There is said to have been a Presbyterian church on this site from the mid 1600s but it was closed in 1672 because of opposition from the civil authorities and the established Anglican church. Presbyterianism first came to the city in the 1640s in the wake of the Scottish forces brought over to Ulster to help quell the rebellion of 1641. It survived despite many obstacles and official disapproval. However after the Siege, Queen Mary gave money to build a church here in gratitude for the bravery of the Presbyterians of the city. In 1780 that church was replaced by the present building. This has undergone many renovations including the addition of the elegant roman corinthian portico in 1903.

PAT COWLEY

L

Name and Address	Telephone

CITY WALLS FROM ELMWOOD TERRACE

The City Walls were built between 1613 and 1618. Londonderry was the last city in Ireland to be encircled by walls. It is the only city on the island where the ancient walls survive almost intact, although it is difficult to get a comprehensive view of them. However, from the Creggan area or here at Elmwood Terrace in the Bogside on the western side of the city, the removal of later buildings make it possible to look at the massively fortified hilltop city. The view here today of the walls is much the same as they would have appeared when the city was built in the early 17th century during the time of the Plantations in Ulster.

With thanks to K. McDaid

PAT COWLEY

Name and Address	*Telephone*

MAGEE COLLEGE

Magee College was originally opened in 1865 as a Presbyterian theological and liberal arts college. It is named after Mrs. Martha Magee whose bequest of £20 000 enabled the project to get off the ground. Mrs Magee was the wife of a Dublin minister and for a long time Magee had a close relationship with Trinity College in Dublin. In the late 1960s the college became part of the New University of Ulster and was somewhat overshadowed for a time by its younger sister institution at Coleraine, but since the mid 1980s the college has undergone a remarkable renaissance and now plays a major role in the expanded University of Ulster.

With thanks to W. A. Caldwell & Co.

PAT CONLEY

Name and Address	Telephone

AUSTINS DEPARTMENT STORE

Although many cities are losing their elegant locally-owned department stores, Derry is lucky that Austins survives as one of the citys' best-known shopping institutions. Built in 1906 following a disastrous fire at its predecessor, (which also destroyed the former Corporation Hall in the centre of the Diamond) it claims to be the oldest such store in the country. The external appearance of the store is in a flamboyant Edwardian design and the tower and cupola on top of the building can be seen from near and far, especially when elaborately lit up at Christmas time. The views over the city and nearby countryside from the restaurant on the top floor are stupendous.

With thanks to Austin & Co.

PAT COWLEY

Name and Address   Telephone

WAPPING LANE

One of the city's oldest districts, and closely-knit communities, is the Wapping or Fountain area. This area huddles close-up beneath, but outside the south-east section of the city walls, adjacent to St. Columb's Cathedral. The name 'Wapping' is probably borrowed from the area in London which lies alongside the river, while the name 'Fountain' may well derive from a water source originally located in this area. As the city began to expand beyond its walls, especially from the early 19th century, the working class communities began to settle in areas with a strongly denominational character. The Wapping or Fountain district became predominantly Protestant in character.

With thanks to the Corner Shop / City Gas and Fuels

PAT COWLEY

Name and Address	Telephone

ST. COLUMB'S CATHEDRAL

St. Columb's is the Church of Ireland cathedral of the Diocese of Derry. It was built between 1628 and 1633 at a cost of about £4000 and was thus the first purpose-built cathedral erected anywhere in these islands following the Reformation. The cathedral has been remodelled and enlarged on several occasions, most notably with the addition of an extended chancel and a chapter house. The latter houses a small museum which contains many objects associated with the general history of the city, especially relating to the Siege of 1689, the Earl Bishop and the famous hymn writer, Mrs. Alexander, whose husband was Bishop here from 1867 to 1896.

Name and Address	Telephone

SHIPQUAY STREET AND THE GUILDHALL

Shipquay Street was the main street of the walled plantation city. Beyond the gate at the bottom of the street was the original ship quay. Gradually the quays were pushed further out into the river and the intervening land reclaimed. It was on such reclaimed land that the new city hall was built in 1890. Named the Guildhall, it was destroyed in an accidental fire in 1908 but was rebuilt in a slightly more elaborate style. Badly damaged in two bomb blasts in 1972, it is now fully operational again as the seat of the City Council and the venue for a whole variety of civic and public events. Its famous 'Big Ben' style clock is said to be the biggest in Ireland.

With thanks to Derry City Council

Name and Address   *Telephone*

THE TOWER MUSEUM

The most obvious external aspect of the Tower Museum, which opened in 1992, is the O'Doherty Tower, built in 1986 in the form of a typical Irish tower house. It is similar in style to a castle erected in this area in the middle ages by the O'Dohertys for their overlords, the O'Donnells, on land bought from the Mac Lochlainn family for 20 cows. The Tower Museum has the unique distinction of winning both the Irish and British 'Museum of the Year' awards. Its main exhibition tells the dramatic story of the development of the city and the tower will eventually house a display of Spanish Armada artifacts, recovered from the ship La Trinidad Valencera by the City of Derry Sub-Aqua Club.

With thanks to Derry City Council

Name and Address	Telephone

CRAIGAVON BRIDGE

Until 1790 the only way to cross the River Foyle was by ferry. In that year a wooden bridge built by two Boston engineers was opened for traffic. That bridge became redundant in 1863 when the Carlisle Bridge was opened a little further upstream. Like its successor, the Carlisle Bridge was a two-tier structure, the lower deck being used to connect up the city's railway termini which by the beginning of this century numbered four. In 1933 the Craigavon Bridge, which had been built alongside the Carlisle Bridge, was opened and the latter was dismantled. The bridge was named after Lord Craigavon, who as Sir James Craig had been the first Prime Minister of Northern Ireland.

With thanks to Shipquay Books Ltd.

PAT COWLEY

Name and Address	Telephone

RAILWAY MUSEUM

By 1900 Derry had four separate railway networks terminating in the city. There were two standard gauge companies: the Great Northern and the Midland, and two narrow gauge companies: the County Donegal Railway and the Londonderry and Lough Swilly Railway. The four systems, plus a small dockside railway, were linked via the lower 'railway' deck of the unusual two-tier bridge. This railway tradition is kept alive by the members of the North West of Ireland Railway Society and by the City Council which in 1989 opened the Foyle Valley Railway, a museum which has its own riverside railway along a two-mile stretch of the former Great Northern permanent way.

With Thanks to The Whatnot

Name and Address	Telephone

THE LINENHALL BAR

Just inside the historic Ferryquay Gate near the top of Market Street is the Linenhall Bar, a free house which still sells all brands of ales and spirits. Its well kept, award winning, frontage is one of the most outstanding barfronts in Derry. There has been a public house on this site for over 100 years and, although the building has been reconstructed and renovated on many occasions, some of the original timbers from the early 18th century are still incorporated. The pub takes its name from the old linenhall which was established nearby in 1759. Local farmers would bring their woven linen to the twice weekly sales where great quantities of the cloth were sold.

With thanks to The Linenhall

PAT COWLEY

Name and Address	Telephone

THE FAUGHAN RIVER

The Faughan river rises in the foothills of the Sperrins on the slopes of Sawel and Learmount mountains. From there it meanders in a north-westerly direction for about 20 miles, flowing past Park, Claudy and Ardmore where the bleach green, redundant old mill buildings and a half hidden mass rock can be found along its banks. Passing Drumahoe, where it flows under the main road to Belfast, the river makes a right turn to flow parallel to the Foyle for several miles before entering Lough Foyle between Coolkeeragh and Donnybrewer. The Faughan is a favourite haunt for the city's fishermen, salmon and sea trout being caught plentifully here during the summer and autumn.

With thanks to Reggie's Seafood Restaurant

PAT COWLEY

Name and Address	*Telephone*

ST. EUGENE'S CATHEDRAL

Work on this building was begun in 1851 by the recently appointed Catholic bishop, Dr. Francis Kelly, who also responsible for introducing a number of welfare and educational institutions to the city such as the Irish Christian Brothers, the Sisters of Mercy and the Society of St. Vincent de Paul. The cathedral is dedicated to St. Eugene (Irish Eoghan) who was the founder of the ancient church of Ardstraw in Co. Tyrone, the first seat of the bishopric which subsequently evolved to become the diocese of Derry. The cathedral was opened in 1873 but it was another thirty years before it acquired its marvellous 256 ft. tall spire.

PAT COWLEY

Name and Address	Telephone

LONDON STREET

Londonderry was the earliest piece of whole city planning in Ireland and its design may well have been derived from the renaissance city of Vitry-le-Francois in eastern France. The geometric grid pattern, according to which the 17th century streets were laid out within the walls, was markedly different to the erratic street plans of older medieval towns. This type of urban planning was ultimately derived from the regular patterns of ancient Roman settlements. The particularly pretty London Street is a typical example of the small side streets which lead off the wide main thoroughfares. It passes the ornate main entrance gates to St. Columb's Cathedral and ends at Newgate.

With thanks to Gordon Galleries

PAT COWLEY

Name and Address   *Telephone*

NESS WOOD WATERFALL

This magnificent waterfall is situated on the Burntollet River a mile or so above the junction where it joins up with the River Faughan. The waterfall is the grand finale of a natural drama in which the river plunges down through a steep, narrow gorge, in a series of steps and cascades, before widening out onto the valley floor. The surrounding slopes are covered with mature trees and shrubs, home to an extensive range of wildlife. The name 'Ness' derives from the Irish words An Eas (literally, the waterfall). At the top of the fall is Shaun's Leap, where the notorious 18th century outlaw, Shaun Crossan, is said to have jumped across the dangerous river rather than be caught by his pursuers.

With thanks to Ness Nurseries & Daisy Chain

PAT COWLEY

Name and Address   *Telephone*

THE DIAMOND AND WAR MEMORIAL

Like most towns which originated during the Plantations in Ulster in the early 17th century, the central square of Derry is known as 'The Diamond'. It has been a market-place, a place of public punishment, a venue for political and religious meetings and a parade ground for ceremonial occasions. The first city hall was built here in 1622. It was destroyed during the Siege but its successor, also known as 'Their Majesties Exchange', was rebuilt in 1692 and continued in use until the Guildhall was built in 1890. For a short time there was a formal garden in the centre of the square but in 1927 the War Memorial by the sculptor Vernon March was erected here.

With thanks to T. & E. Howie

Name and Address	Telephone

THE DEANERY, BISHOP STREET

The Deanery is one of the finest Georgian style buildings surviving in the city. It is located close to St. Columb's Cathedral in Bishop Street (within the walls) beside a number of other public or former public buildings. As its name implies, it is the home of the Dean of the Cathedral. It is a three-storey over basement town-house with a fine brick frontage and a beautiful doorway approached up a short flight of stone steps. Although its architectural style is older, the house was built in 1833. Derry has had many distinguished deans, among them the famous philosopher, George Berkeley. He was appointed in 1724 and remained in office until 1732 although he seldom stayed in the city.

With thanks to Brendan Kearney Kelly & Co.

Local Directory
& Sponsors

We would like to express our sincere thanks
to the following businesses and organisations
without whose help and support this book
would not have been possible.

BUSINESS NAME AND ADDRESS	TEL	FAX
Antiques & Collectables		
THE WHATNOT		
22 BISHOP STREET	265008	
Art Gallery		
THE MCGILLOWAY GALLERY		
6 SHIPQUAY STREET	366011	
Bookshop		
BOOKWORM COMMUNITY BOOKSHOP		
18-20 BISHOP STREET	261616	361327
Bookshop & Newsagent		
SHIPQUAY BOOKS LIMITED		
10 SHIPQUAY STREET	371747	
Charity		
THE HONOURABLE THE IRISH SOCIETY		
54 CASTLEROE ROAD, COLERAINE (01265)	44796	56527
Department Store		
AUSTIN & CO.		
THE DIAMOND	261817	370124
Dress & Furnishing Fabrics, Haberdashery, Crafts and Gifts		
MOORE'S OF DERRY		
FERRYQUAY GATE, CARLISLE ROAD	262777	
Fine Art Dealers & Picture Framers, Fine Crafts		
GORDON GALLERIES		
7 LONDON STREET	374044	374044
Garden Centre/Florist		
NESS NURSERIES & DAISY CHAIN		
234 GLENSHANE ROAD	301285	301581
General Store & Gas Distribution		
CORNER SHOP / CITY GAS & FUELS		
1 AUBERY STREET	267394	269339
Insurance Consultants		
W. A. CALDWELL & CO		
24 NORTHLAND ROAD	364267	

Business Name and Address	Tel	Fax
Jewellery, Furniture, Giftware, Leather Goods, Post Office & Coffee Shop		
T. & E. Howie		
The Diamond	262168	261978
Local Economic Development		
Derry Boston Ventures Limited, t/a North West International		
1 St. Columb's Court	371722	268976
Local Government		
Derry City Council		
Guildhall	365151	264858
Newsagent & Confectionery		
K McDaid		
43 Elmwood Terrace	268324	
Office Equipment & Artist's Materials		
L.P.C. Stationery		
5 Bishop Street	261921	360143
Public House & Restaurant		
The Linenhall		
3 Market Street	371665	372237
Seafood Restaurant & Wet Fish Shop		
Reggie's Seafood Restaurant		
145B Strand Road	262050	
Shopping Centre		
The Richmond Centre		
Richmond Centre	260525	373402
Solicitors		
Brendan Kearney Kelly & Co. (Solicitors)		
Clarendon House, 4 Clarendon Street	266935	371845
Toys & Nursery		
Hills (Derry) Limited		
39/43 Spencer Road	42001	48648
Watchmaker & Jeweller		
W. J. Sproule		
26 Carlisle Road	266994	

Open Diary

This section is provided to record personal
dates such as birthdays, anniversaries and
other important annual events.

January

1 ....

2 ....

3 ....

4 ....

5 ....

6 ....

7 ....

8 ....

9 ....

10 ....

11 ....

12 ....

13 ....

14 ....

15 ....

16 ....

17 ....

18 ....

19 ....

20 ....

21 ....

22 ....

23 ....

24 ....

25 ....

26 ....

27 ....

28 ....

29 ....

30 ....

31 ....

February

1	*16*
2	*17*
3	*18*
4	*19*
5	*20*
6	*21*
7	*22*
8	*23*
9	*24*
10	*25*
11	*26*
12	*27*
13	*28*
14	*29*
15	

March

1	*16*
2	*17*
3	*18*
4	*19*
5	*20*
6	*21*
7	*22*
8	*23*
9	*24*
10	*25*
11	*26*
12	*27*
13	*28*
14	*29*
15	*30*
	31

April

1	*16*
2	*17*
3	*18*
4	*19*
5	*20*
6	*21*
7	*22*
8	*23*
9	*24*
10	*25*
11	*26*
12	*27*
13	*28*
14	*29*
15	*30*

May

1	*16*
2	*17*
3	*18*
4	*19*
5	*20*
6	*21*
7	*22*
8	*23*
9	*24*
10	*25*
11	*26*
12	*27*
13	*28*
14	*29*
15	*30*
	31

June

1	16
2	17
3	18
4	19
5	20
6	21
7	22
8	23
9	24
10	25
11	26
12	27
13	28
14	29
15	30

July

1	16
2	17
3	18
4	19
5	20
6	21
7	22
8	23
9	24
10	25
11	26
12	27
13	28
14	29
15	30
	31

August

1	16
2	17
3	18
4	19
5	20
6	21
7	22
8	23
9	24
10	25
11	26
12	27
13	28
14	29
15	30
	31

September

1	*16*
2	*17*
3	*18*
4	*19*
5	*20*
6	*21*
7	*22*
8	*23*
9	*24*
10	*25*
11	*26*
12	*27*
13	*28*
14	*29*
15	*30*

October

1		16	
2		17	
3		18	
4		19	
5		20	
6		21	
7		22	
8		23	
9		24	
10		25	
11		26	
12		27	
13		28	
14		29	
15		30	
		31	

November

1	*16*
2	*17*
3	*18*
4	*19*
5	*20*
6	*21*
7	*22*
8	*23*
9	*24*
10	*25*
11	*26*
12	*27*
13	*28*
14	*29*
15	*30*

December

1	*16*
2	*17*
3	*18*
4	*19*
5	*20*
6	*21*
7	*22*
8	*23*
9	*24*
10	*25*
11	*26*
12	*27*
13	*28*
14	*29*
15	*30*
	31

Cottage

Publications

Dear Reader

We hope you have found this book both enjoyable and useful. If you feel that it could have been improved in any way do please let us know.

This book is one of our 'Illustrated History and Companion' range. Other towns and areas currently featured in this range include:–

Ballycastle and the Heart of the Glens
Ballymena
Ballymoney
Bangor
Coleraine and the Causeway Coast
Donaghadee
Hillsborough
Holywood
Larne and the Road to the Glens
Newtownards

If you require more information call us on 01247 883876 or write to:– **Cottage Publications**
15 Ballyhay Road
Donaghadee, Co. Down
N. Ireland
BT21 0NG

Timothy S Johnston